The Urbana Free Library

To renew: call 217-367-4057
or go to *"urbanafreelibrary.org"*
and select "Renew/Request Items"

RAT

Karen Latchana Kenney

Rourke
Educational Media

rourkeeducationalmedia.com

Before Reading:

Building Academic Vocabulary and Background Knowledge

Before reading a book, it is important to tap into what your child or students already know about the topic. This will help them develop their vocabulary, increase their reading comprehension, and make connections across the curriculum.

1. *Look at the cover of the book. What will this book be about?*
2. *What do you already know about the topic?*
3. *Let's study the Table of Contents. What will you learn about in the book's chapters?*
4. *What would you like to learn about this topic? Do you think you might learn about it from this book? Why or why not?*
5. *Use a reading journal to write about your knowledge of this topic. Record what you already know about the topic and what you hope to learn about the topic.*
6. *Read the book.*
7. *In your reading journal, record what you learned about the topic and your response to the book.*
8. *After reading the book complete the activities below.*

Content Area Vocabulary
Read the list. What do these words mean?

bedding
bonds
breeder
exotic
feces
gnaw
laboratories
mammal
mites
nocturnal
scavenge
urine
veterinarian

After Reading:

Comprehension and Extension Activity

After reading the book, work on the following questions with your child or students in order to check their level of reading comprehension and content mastery.

1. *Would a pet rat be a good fit for your family? Explain. (Text to self connection)*
2. *Why are some people afraid of rats? (Asking questions)*
3. *How did rats become so plentiful around the world? Explain. (Infer)*
4. *In what ways are pet rats like cats and dogs? (Summarize)*
5. *What are some ways you can prepare your home for your pet rat? (Asking questions)*

Extension Activity

Rats are used in laboratories to test various products such as medications and cosmetics. Do you agree or disagree with animal testing? Research animal testing with rats and create a presentation supporting your opinion.

Table of Contents

Rainforest Rat..4

Rats: Head to Toe..8

Popular Pets 10

Buying Pet Rats...16

Staying Healthy 24

Glossary 30

Index..31

Show What You Know 31

Websites to Visit 31

About the Author 32

Rainforest Rat

A giant white-tailed rat stirs in its log den. Its home is in the rainforest of Australia.

At night, the wild rat begins its search for food. The **nocturnal mammal** climbs up tall trees. Coconuts are one of its favorite foods. The rat's sharp teeth are perfect tools. It can easily **gnaw** into tough coconut shells.

Both wild and pet rats are clever animals. That's one reason rats can be interesting pets.

FUN FACT

The giant white-tailed rat is big! It's one of the biggest rodents in Australia. It can weigh more than 1.8 pounds (800 grams).

Wild Rats

You can find rats in remote places such as rainforests. But this mammal also lives close to humans. They live in trees, by water, in caves, and in buildings.

Near people, wild rats eat nearly everything. They **scavenge** for food in the trash. In nature, brown rats prefer meat. They like snails, fish, and rabbits. Rainforest rats eat fruit and seeds. Other rats eat insects and worms.

Rats live in large groups called colonies. Females have about eight babies at a time. Each is hairless and blind at first. The babies' eyes open after 14 days.

Rat Origins

Rats originally came from Asia, Australia, and nearby islands. Many rats spread to other parts of the world on explorers' ships.

Rats: Head to Toe

You can tell a rat from other rodents by its tail. It looks smooth and bare, but it's not. It has short, fine hair. Hair covers the rest of its body, too. Most rats weigh between 3.4 and 8.5 ounces (95 to 240 grams). Their bodies are 6.7 to 8.3 inches (17 to 21 centimeters) long. Many rats' tails stretch as long as their bodies.

This small animal has many features that help it thrive in the wild.

A long tail helps rats balance as they climb.

Sharp claws and long legs help rats jump, run, and climb. Some jump up to 3 feet (0.9 meters) high! Sharp claws grip trees, wires, and buildings.

Rats have excellent hearing and sense of smell. They help rats find food.

Rats can see up to 40 feet (12.2 meters) away at night but they cannot see colors.

A rat's whiskers are always moving and touching. They help rats know what is around them.

Rats have four large, sharp teeth. They gnaw into tough materials. Twelve molars grind food. Their teeth never stop growing.

Popular Pets

A pet rat is called a fancy rat. Many people love their pet rats. They are smaller than wild rats. They are calmer and friendlier, too.

Fancy rats come in different varieties. Some have curly hair or large ears. Others don't have hair or tails. Their fur may have different colors and patterns.

Pet rats love attention. They form strong **bonds** with their owners. It's what makes them such popular pets.

FUN FACT

Fancy rats were first bred in the late 1800s. In the 1900s it became popular to keep rats as pets.

Are you ready to be a rat owner? Rats are pretty easy to care for. They are small, quiet pets. But they do need regular attention. Can you keep its cage clean? Can you give it fresh water and food every day?

These social animals need to play. They need to explore outside of their cages, too. Can you buy more than one rat? It's best to have a few. Single rats can become stressed and lonely. Do you have time to spend with a pet rat? A rat needs several hours of attention each day.

FUN FACT

An Indian temple was built for the Hindu rat goddess. It is the Karni Mata temple. About 20,000 rats live there!

▶▶ *The rats at the Karni Mata Temple are called kabbas. They are considered holy animals. People travel from all over the world to visit and pay their respects.*

13

Some Owner Risks

Is anyone in your home allergic to rats? Some people get rashes from rat **urine**. A pet rat leaves urine and **feces** as it explores your home. You must clean up after it.

Remember, rats love to chew! At home, this might be a problem. A pet rat could chew on wood, plastic, paper, cords, and fabric. Be prepared to rat-proof your home.

Rats can bite if they get scared, but this is rare. Also, pet rats have a short lifespan. Most live only two to two and one-half years. It can be hard to lose your pet so soon.

Symptoms of an allergic reaction to a pet rat include a runny nose, hives or skin welts, itchy throat and wheezing.

15

Buying Pet Rats

You can buy pet rats from several places. Pet shops usually sell rats. Animal shelters may have unwanted rats. **Laboratories** sometimes give away their extra rats. A **breeder** may sell unusual rats. Or other owners' rats may have babies. They may sell or give away the babies.

Pick a rat that is four to six weeks old. It will adapt better to being your pet. Look for one that is healthy and active. A shiny coat and bright eyes are good signs. Females tend to be more active. Males are less active. They may sit on your lap longer. If buying two rats, check the genders! You may end up with a lot of baby rats if you buy a male and female.

PET POINTERS
Some laboratories test chemicals on rats. The rats they use are the same kind as pet rats.

17

Your Pet Rat

Before you bring your pet home, you need to prepare. First, buy a good cage and set it up.

You can choose between a wire cage and an aquarium. A wire cage lets in more air. A pan at the bottom can be pulled out for cleaning. An aquarium needs more cleaning. It traps more dirt inside. Your pet rat's home should be at least as big as a 10-gallon (38 liter) aquarium.

wire cage

aquarium

Place litter at the bottom of the cage. It traps urine and feces. Do not use pine or cedar, though. Their oils harm rats. Try rabbit food, aspen wood shavings, or shredded paper. Use paper without ink.

Pet Pointers

Rats like to sleep in a nest box. A plastic or cardboard container works. In the winter put **bedding** inside. Strips of paper towels or tissues make good bedding.

The Right Diet

Clean water and fresh food are very important. Use a water bottle with a sipper tube. Hang it on the side of your pet's cage. Clean the bottle daily and fill it with fresh water.

A heavy ceramic dish is good for food. Rats chew on plastic dishes. Buy rodent blocks at pet stores. This is a special food made for rats. Add some fresh fruit and vegetables. Remove leftover food each day. It will go bad if left in the cage and make your pet rat sick.

Pet Pointers

Adult rats should eat 80 percent rodent blocks and 20 percent fresh food.

Toys and Play

   Curious and active rats love to play.
When owners are not around, rats play
with toys. They climb over and under
things. Tubes, ropes, ladders, and sticks
are great for climbing. Rats love exercise
wheels, too. Choose one at least 10
inches (25 centimeters) across.

You can make fun toys for your pet rat. Tape small cardboard boxes together to make a playhouse. Build a maze with cardboard tubes and plastic pipes. Put a treat at the end. Smart rats quickly find their way through mazes.

Staying Healthy

Rats are clean animals. They groom themselves. But owners should brush their rats once a day. Brushing removes dead skin, bedding, and dirt from a rat's fur. Trim its nails every six to eight weeks. Be sure to check and clean a rat's ears, too. **Mites** can infest their ears.

Pet Pointers

Sometimes rats eat their droppings. It may seem gross but it's actually helpful. They are special droppings that contain B vitamins and good bacteria.

A sick rat needs to see a **veterinarian** who treats **exotic** animals. Watch your pet for signs of an illness. Does your rat look scruffy? Is it losing hair? Is it tired all the time? Is it not eating or drinking? If so, your pet may be sick.

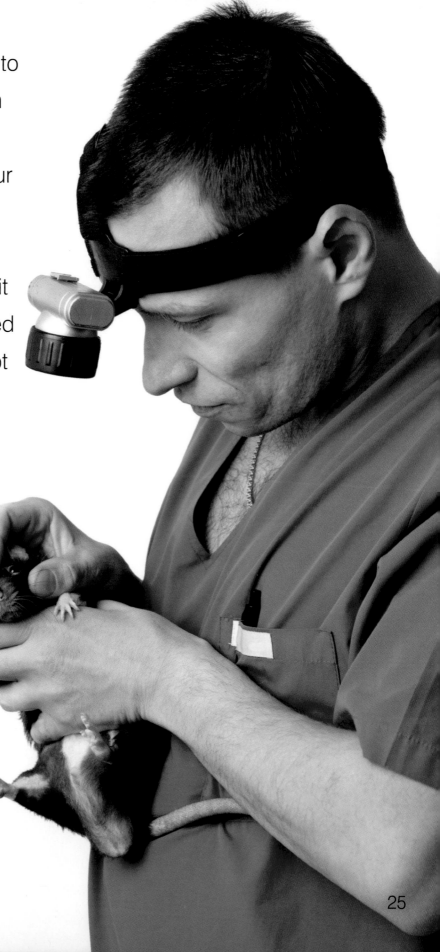

Bonding with Owners

A new rat needs a few days to adjust. Give it some space. It may be scared. Then offer it some treats. The rat will know its owner's smell. It will become friendlier.

Now it is time to be social. Spend time with a pet rat each day. Pet its fur. Feed it small bits of food from your hand. It will soon run to its owner for attention.

Many rats learn tricks. Rats run when they hear their names called. They climb or sit up on command. Rats can even be trained to use a litter box, just like a cat.

Friendly and Curious Rats

Some people have negative opinions about rats. They only know what wild rats can do. But pet rats are very different. They run through difficult mazes. They get excited to see their owners. And they come when called, like a little dog. Give your pet rat love and attention. It will be a wonderful addition to your family.

Things to Think About If You Want a Pet Rat

- Pet rats only live up to two and one-half years.
- They need a few hours of attention each day.
- Rats eat special food from a pet store. They also need fresh fruits and vegetables.
- Its cage, food bowl, and water bottle need to be kept clean.
- Some people are allergic to rat urine.

Glossary

bedding (BED-ing): material used for animals to cushion their bodies and absorb smells and wetness

bonds (BONDZ): forms close connections

breeder (BREED-ur): a person who keeps, mates, and sells animals

exotic (eg-ZOT-ic): in animals, one that is native to another country

feces (FEE-sees): the solid droppings of animals

gnaw (NAW): to keep biting something

laboratories (LAB-ruh-tor-eez): rooms, buildings, or institutes people use to conduct science experiments

mammal (MAM-uhl): a warm-blooded animal with a spine, whose females produce milk for their young

mites (MITES): tiny animals with eight legs that are related to spiders

nocturnal (nok-TUR-nuhl): to be active at night

scavenge (SKAV-uhnj): to search in garbage for food or useful things

urine (YOOR-uhn): the liquid waste of animals

veterinarian (vet-ur-uh-NER-ee-uhn): a doctor who treats sick animals

Index

bodies 8, 9

bonding 10, 26

breeder 16

cages 18, 19, 20

care 12, 14, 26

diet 20, 21

habitat 4, 6, 7

laboratories 16, 17

lifespan 14

risks 14

sickness 20, 25

social groups 6

toys 22, 23

Show What You Know

1. Where do wild rats originally come from?

2. How many babies do rats have at a time?

3. When were fancy rats first bred?

4. What can rat urine do to some people?

5. What kind of cage should you buy for a pet rat?

Websites to Visit

www.afrma.org/kidsguide.htm

www.abc.net.au/creaturefeatures/facts/rats.htm

www.biokids.umich.edu/critters/Rattus_norvegicus

About the Author

Karen Latchana Kenney is the author of more than 100 books for children. She's written about all kinds of animals—from the tiny bee hummingbird to the spiny sea urchin. Kenney lives and works in Minneapolis, Minnesota.

Meet The Author!
www.meetREMauthors.com

www.rourkeeducationalmedia.com

PHOTO CREDITS: Cover, page 3, page 16, page 23 (left), page 25: ©Dmitry Maslov; page 1: ©Pakhnyushchyy; page 5: ©bikeriderlondon; page 6 (top): ©Andrew_Howe; page 6 (bottom): ©lifeonwhote.com; page 7: ©miniature; page 8: ©Antagain; page 9: ©wildcat78; page 10: ©NoDerog; page 12: ©Ilya731; page 13 (top): ©Rafal Cichawa; page 13: ©BremecR; page 15: ©LevebtKonuk; page 17: ©NiDerLander; page 18 (left): ©Mrreporter; page 18 (right): ©DonNicholas; page 19: ©siamionaupavel; page 20: ©TonyWear; page 21, page 23 (right): ©Argument; page 22: ©James Brey; page 24 (left top): ©herreid; page 24 (right top): ©Sychugina Elena; page 24 (left bottom): ©Sohel Parvez Haque; page 26, page 28: ©Liudmila P. Sundikova; page 29: ©Nadezda S. Sundikova; page 30: ©GlobalIP

Edited by: Keli Sipperley

Cover design and Interior design by: Rhea Magaro

Library of Congress PCN Data

Rat / Karen Latchana Kenney
(You Have a Pet What?!)
ISBN 978-1-63430-435-1 (hard cover)
ISBN 978-1-63430-535-8 (soft cover)
ISBN 978-1-63430-624-9 (e-Book)
Library of Congress Control Number: 2015931858

Printed in the United States of America, North Mankato, Minnesota

Also Available as:

ROURKE'S
e-Books